From Sunsets To Stars

Words that healed me on the Central Coast

Ben Bence

BookLeaf Publishing

India | USA | UK

Copyright © Ben Bence
All Rights Reserved.

This book has been self-published with all reasonable efforts taken to make the material error-free by the author. No part of this book shall be used, reproduced in any manner whatsoever without written permission from the author, except in the case of brief quotations embodied in critical articles and reviews.

The Author of this book is solely responsible and liable for its content including but not limited to the views, representations, descriptions, statements, information, opinions, and references ["Content"]. The Content of this book shall not constitute or be construed or deemed to reflect the opinion or expression of the Publisher or Editor. Neither the Publisher nor Editor endorse or approve the Content of this book or guarantee the reliability, accuracy, or completeness of the Content published herein and do not make any representations or warranties of any kind, express or implied, including but not limited to the implied warranties of merchantability, fitness for a particular purpose.

The Publisher and Editor shall not be liable whatsoever...

Made with ❤ on the BookLeaf Publishing Platform
www.bookleafpub.in
www.bookleafpub.com

Dedication

Dear everyone I've ever met,
I don't know if I ever cross your mind.
Or how many times you appear in mine.
I hope I brought blue to your skies.
I'm sorry if I ever left tears in your eyes.
I will always try to do better.
You will forever matter to me.
I'll always want the best for you,
If you need anything come find me too.
Big or small I'm thankful for your part in my life.
I wouldn't be me if it wasn't for your light.

Preface

Similar to most people in the world, during the COVID-19 pandemic, my world turned upside down. When faced with fear and isolation, you are forced to either reflect or hide. I chose to reflect, tear apart my life and start over. After being laid off from what was a dream job (at the time), I left a longterm relationship, moved out of my parent's house and focused full-time on my mental health. This involved seeking care, time on my paddle board, hiking most importantly, seeing sunsets along the central coast of California. I would watch sunsets become stars, meditate, reflect and write. Through my writing, I was able to feel, to hurt and to heal.

This is a collection of twenty-one poems from my healing journey to showcase my early work.

I hope you enjoy,

Ben

Acknowledgements

I would like to thank the land and it's ancestors for having me, for holding me and for healing me. These poems were written in modern day Monterey, Big Sur, Carmel, Pacific Grove, and Marina. This land originally stewarded by the Esselen, Rumsen, Costanoan and Ohlone people.

This writing was made possible because of teachers like my 6th grade English teacher, Sandra Shepherd. Up until then, I had no belief in myself as a student. I had zero academic confidence and never even considered my writing ability. Ms. Shepherd changed all that for me, through kindness, patience and support. she is a major reason I'm currently a teacher.

Thank you to my great love, my fiancé Monica Gonzalez. Her perfectly matched love for me many years later after writing these poems is a testament of what putting in the hard work of heeling can be. Her support and belief in me inspired me to publish. To my three-month-old, Olympia, I put in all this work for you. To learn from my mistakes and be the best father I could possibly be.

Journey of Self

In this game of life I can be an imposter.
Reflect positivity and absorb such doubt.
I'm not sure if I'm a hero of my own growth,
or a prisoner of my mistakes.

Resilience, it comes in waves.
Am I a strong enough surfer for the next set of swell?

Hope is high like mountain peaks,
perseverance is that hike to reach.
Dreams are the stars above,
some nights too covered to see,
on the clearest, too many to achieve.

So where do I start?
Which star do I pick?
Mountain do I climb or wave do I ride?
This is probably not up to me to decide.
This journey of self, is alive.

Mindfulness

I do not ever wish for time to stand still.
There is magic in the consistent spontaneity of reactions
that we measure in moments.
Instead, I'll stand still in time.
Together, we can coexist in the present.
Absorb and share this intimate moment of existence, as
it's being created.
This feeling is mindfulness.
What it truly feels like to be alive.
A partnership with time,
an understanding of place,
how life is a sweet harmony of everything.

I often look back or forward in time
Not realizing the present is what life truly is.
It's too easy to let slip by.
Too important not to stop and realize.

Humbled Hillsides

Broken down so much
you've become sand on the beach.
Once a tall bolder,
you now bring quiet and peace.

Even the most beaten down rocks become smooth sand
that bring beauty and peace,
despite their violent history.
Leaving behind pieces of themselves each step of the
way,
unnecessary weight they carried until they reach their
final form.
All that they ever needed to be,
at the bottom of the beach,

I bet here too they are most at peace.
Given what they've felt and seen.

Hillsides humbled to grains,
Yet they remain the same.

Angry Sea

Oh sea, oh sea.
Why are you so angry?
Showing your power
Where you usually do your beauty.

Winds so strong,
I cannot stand tall.

They say never turn your back to the sea.
However, I have no choice with this weather
The sand stings skin and aims for the eyes.
I realize,
I'm bowed down at your raging waves
Is this the day you take me?

Big Sur Screams

The Big Sur siren singsa beautifully frightening wallow
of warning.
In a moan of pain from her abduction,
through the wind in a cry of sorrow,
She begs me to protect this sacred land.
Warning me of the woes the steep cliffs and sharp hills
may otherwise bring.

Rain on the Roof

The rain rolls off my roof,
reminding me of last year in my little room.
The peaceful song of little taps,
like a loved one gently waking you up from a nap.
With each drop of rain,
I imagined my pain washing away.

Home

What is home?
A place that you live?
Or a place where you are from?
I dance these winding trails of wildflowers in the golden
hour glow,
Sit on the beach,
And know
This is home.

Monterey Morning

The sunshine pours through the pillars,
kisses the water and lights up the trees.

The fog rolls away to set up a clear day.
The waves rock in a way that would make the most
comforting chair jealous.
Is this not heaven?
This is my paradise.
There's no need to look forward to an afterlife.
Because every Monterey morning
I'm born again.

Eye to Eye with the Mountainside

I'm eye to eye with the top side of the mountain.
I've made it to the canopy of the redwood trees,
I see the ocean and ridges going endlessly,
as the vultures and hawks pass by my head
I see the perspective from the way they live.

I have to catch my breath thrice.
Once from the slope and twice from the beauty.
It's worth the sweat, the last drop of water in this bottle,
the racing of my heart and the burning in my body.
I'm in control of myself.

What is God?

Is God the mutual star in all of us?
From where all life and matter began.
Is that why I feel so connected to the stars and the sea?
Why the universe pulls me,
or that I can feel a trees energy?
Why I feel the same looking at the night sky
As I do in your eyes?
Does everything trace back to the star that is God?

Around the Corner

I am watching bats chase flies
as it begins to become night,
by a river that's usually blocked off by the sea .
Who knew that this paradise was just around the corner,
waiting for the right time to be seen.
Be patient and you'll get what you need.

Coffee Cup

I saw my reflection on the bottom of my coffee cup.
For the first time in a while, I feel like I'm enough.
I saw the peace and calm in my eyes,
I felt the warmth inside.
This time it's a mix of the sun waking up,
the drink in my cup,
and knowing I'm enough.

Catastrophic Molt

I've overcome my catastrophic molt.
I may appear the same, however I've grown.
Looks are deceiving, I'm not the same.
I shed the imprint of who I was.

Overcame the necessary risk and vulnerability of being
brittle to reach the reward of strength.

My shell is now strong and not so new.
The walls of my soul are no longer closing in.
Though painful, the growth set me free.
It's time to begin life in this case,
One I will carry for the rest of time
now knowing it's truly mine.

Change with Rain

The rain came on this momentous day,
to wash away the pain of yesterday.
I fall asleep to the gentle sound of change,
knowing I'll wake up having truly found,
the strength to get my feet off the ground.

I found peace like the smell of wet pine trees.
I found hope and fell like leaves in the wind.
Making way for next seasons growth,
this time It will stand tall and evergreen.
No storm will be too big.
I'm ready to truly live.

Electricity

My body flows with the electricity called passion.
An energy that curates not a lightbulb idea,
But powers gridlines of innovation.

I feel it in my bones.
As if a lightning strike of creativity restarts my heart,
Pulses ways to change through my veins.

Some say they see the gears turning,
Well, I feel the waves flowing.
Each thought a raindrop,
onto the river of ideas.
Leading to the ocean of outcomes
A sea far too deep to ever get empty.

Metamorphosis

I can feel the change
bursting through my veins.
I climbed up that cliff to reminisce.
My wings ready to unfold,
This is my metamorphosis.
The pain of their growth had the little bits of salty life
escape from my eyes.

The last time I saw this sight,
I was a different guy.
This is not where he would be,
when last up here asked in five years
What do you see?

Here I am on the path meant to be,
with feelings I've never experienced.
So content and free,
it terrified me.
My soul remains the same.
Now with wings, I'm ready to soar into my true self.

17. Bird in the Wind

Sometimes I feel like a bird in the wind.
I can only decide where I begin, not where I'll end up.
I can either try to fight the wind and stay in place,
or I can accept the wind with grace,
soaring in the direction the world has in mind.

CSUMB Library

This library is home to heartbreak.
Long distance loneliness,
Failed exams and courses.
Breakups and class makeups.
Start of a pandemic,
End of friend's lives.
Hairs pulled and brain growth.
Crutches, limps and skips.
Tears of pain, relief and joy.
These cold cement walls, have seen it all.
Watched me prove myself wrong,
turn my dreams into reality.

Summer Solstice

Even wildflowers close off for darkness.
All the colors start to fade.

Poppies go away.
Lupins decay.
With them gone I realize,
that I'm not okay.
Spring is ending,
a summer of sadness starts today.
I'll be here,
the last remaining flower.
Watching all my flower friends fade away.

GO TO YOUR DESIRE

"GO TO YOUR DESIRE. DON'T HANG AROUND HERE"

I read under the moonlight.
Gazing at the moving window in the clouds that felt as if
the past was rolling away too.
I can't help but to wonder what the next clear night sky
will reveal.

To most there are only two directions.
The direction of desire and the direction of destiny.
Well, I desire my destiny and that's already set for me.
So I will go that way instead of hanging around in my
head,
for I trust whatever lies ahead.

Everything

Everything you need to heal
The world provides.
Slow down time.
Close your eyes.
Open them and try.
Try to find each star in the sky.

Listen to the sea applauding
Your every victory.
The sound of birds singing their symphony.
More than ever it's clear to me,
The universe provides peace unconditionally.
We just have open our hearts to the energy

www.ingramcontent.com/pod-product-compliance
Lightning Source LLC
Chambersburg PA
CBHW071246140726
47996CB00007B/2780